Contents

How to use this book

Writing non-fiction

(1) **Definition** – This describes the genre and provides examples of the text type.

(2) **Text type** – Each type of writing is explained in a step-by-step way to help you plan.

(3) **Self-assessment** – Tick the face that best describes your understanding of this concept.

(4) **Text plan** – Planning is very important when writing fiction and non-fiction and these charts will help you plan properly.

(5) **Language features** – This section explains the language features used for this type of text, including examples.

(6) **Text example** – This gives you an example of a well-written piece of text that follows the text plan and contains key language features.

(7) **Commentary** – This highlights the key features of the example text so that you can see how and why it is a good example of the genre.

(8) **Practice questions** – This is where you do the work! Try answering the questions by using the text plan and by referring to the key language features. Compare your work against the written example – is it good enough for Level 5?

(9) **Tips** – Key hints and tips to help you achieve Level 5.

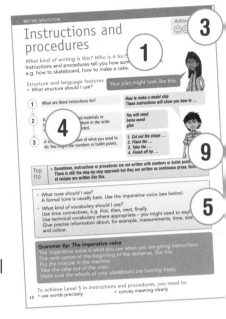

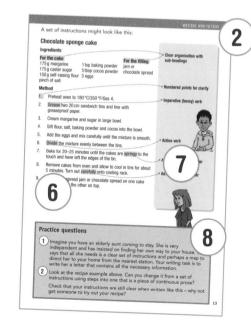

Writing fiction

1 **Structure** – This provides a model structure for your fiction writing including examples.

2 **Setting, character and theme** – This explains the key ingredients for writing fiction and explores each ingredient in depth.

3 **Planning** – This provides you with a structure to use before you begin writing a story.

4 **Challenge** – This gives you a chance to practise your writing skills, including planning.

5 **Tips** – The tips give you ideas and hints to improve your work.

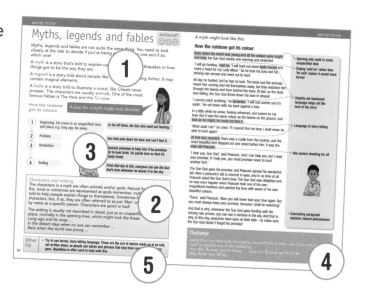

Reading comprehension

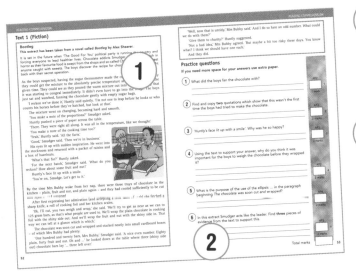

1 **Text examples** – These give you typical examples of a piece of text that you might find in your National Tests.

2 **Questions** – The text is followed by a number of questions relating to it. There are 1-, 2- and 3-mark questions so remember to read between the lines.

In addition you will find over 100 clear tips and facts to help you with:
grammar   spelling   punctuation   vocabulary   handwriting

A glossary of terms can be found on page 59.

If you use this guidance to help you prepare for your test you will have a great chance of achieving Level 5!

About the National Tests

Key facts

★ The Key Stage 2 National Tests take place in the summer term in Year 6. You will be tested on Maths and English.

★ The tests take place in your school and will be marked by examiners – not your teacher!

★ Individual scores are not made public. However, a school's combined scores are published in what are commonly known as 'league tables'.

The National Tests for English

You will take three tests in English. These are designed to test your reading comprehension, grammar, punctuation and spelling. Your writing is now teacher assessed, along with handwriting.

The Reading Test

This is one test to assess your reading comprehension. In this test you will be given a series of texts and an answer booklet. You will have one hour to read the texts and complete the answer booklet section of the test. You use the texts to answer the questions so you do not need to memorise them. You should refer to the texts closely while you are answering. Some of the questions guide you to a particular page, 'Look at page 6,' but you will need to identify the correct text in other questions.

The Grammar, Punctuation and Spelling Test

The grammar and punctuation part of the test lasts 45 minutes. There are different types of questions for you to answer in different ways. For some questions you do not need to do any writing. Instead, they are multiple choice options, ticking the correct answer, drawing lines to, or putting a circle around your answers. It is incredibly important therefore to read the instructions carefully, so that you know how to answer the question. For other questions however, you will need to write a word, phrase or sentence.

The spelling task lasts 15 minutes, although you will be allowed as much time as you need to complete it. Your teacher or another adult will read out twenty sentences. Each sentence has a word missing in the answer booklet. You must listen carefully to the missing word and fill this in, making sure that you spell it correctly. The word will be read out once, then as part of a sentence and then repeated a third and final time.

Test techniques

Before the test

(1) When you revise, try revising a 'little and often' rather than in long sessions.

(2) Read the hints and tips throughout the book to remind you of important points.

(3) Revise with a friend. You can encourage and learn from each other.

(4) Be prepared – bring your own pens and pencils.

During the test

(1) READ THE QUESTION THEN READ IT AGAIN.

(2) If you get stuck, don't linger on the same question – move on! You can come back to it later.

(3) Never leave a multiple choice question. Make an educated guess if you really can't work out the answer.

(4) Check to see how many marks a question is worth. Have you 'earned' those marks with your answer?

(5) Check your answers after each question. Does your answer look correct?

Where to go to get help

Pages 9, 24, 34 and 51 provide you with a description of what you should aim to do when you are reading and writing at Level 5.

Pages 8–33 are designed to help you succeed in the Writing Test and include information about writing fiction and non-fiction.

Pages 34–45 will help you give 'voice' to your writing, sharpen up your punctuation and improve your grammar.

Pages 46–47 give you practice in spelling.

Pages 48–57 are designed to help you succeed in the Reading Test and include reading fiction, non-fiction and poetry.

Page 58 contains the golden rules to improve handwriting.

Page 59 contains a glossary to help you understand key terms about writing, reading and grammar.

Pages 60–63 provide the answers to the practice questions.

Writing non-fiction

There are six main types of non-fiction writing. They are:
- Recount
- Non-chronological report
- Discussion
- Instructions and procedures
- Explanation
- Persuasion

Each type of writing (often called *genres* of writing) has special features; you need to think about what genre you are being asked to write to decide how to do it! It's also useful to decide who the writing is for – in other words, who your *audience* is, because this might make a difference to how you write as well.

> **Rule number 1**
> Before you start to write, always ask yourself:
> - *What kind of writing is this?*
> - *Who is it for?*

You then need to think about the ingredients that go into that genre. Each genre has its own structure and language features. 'Language features' means things like what *tense* you write in, what *tone* you use (e.g. should it be formal or informal? Jokey or serious?) and what kind of *vocabulary* you use.

> **Rule number 2**
> Ask yourself:
> - *What structure should I use?*
> - *What tone should I use?*
> - *What tense should I write in?*
> - *What kind of vocabulary should I use?*

Then plan your writing.

In class, you'll probably talk about planning and have plenty of time to do it. It is always important to make time to plan your writing before you begin.

Think about the shape of the writing you're going to do. Does it matter what order you put things in? What's the most important point you want to make? Is there a good way of starting your writing to grab your readers' attention?

Now is also a good time to jot down any key words or powerful vocabulary you might use.

> **Rule number 3**
> - *Give yourself a moment to plan your writing, even if you have limited time to do it.*

On the following pages, there are examples of all the different non-fiction genres with checklists of their language features, and practice questions for you to try. Remember the three rules!

Achieve Level 5 writing

At Level 5 your writing is varied and interesting. You can convey meaning in a range of forms for different readers and write more formally where this is appropriate. You can make imaginative choices of vocabulary and use words precisely. You can organise simple, compound and complex sentences into paragraphs and use a range of punctuation correctly, including commas, apostrophes and quotation marks. You usually spell words with complex regular patterns correctly. Your handwriting is fluent, joined and clear, and you can adapt it to a range of tasks.

Over to you!

- Work through each section and don't rush.
- Learn the purpose of the text type.
- Make sure you understand the way it is organised and what the key language features are.
- Have a go at the challenges and the practice questions.

Tips	The practice questions	
	★ Decide what the *purpose* of the writing is. This is the clue to which text type to write. E.g. *Write a letter describing a weekend away …* Straight away this tells you the text should be a RECOUNT. *Write a letter to persuade someone to …* Straight away this tells you to write a PERSUASIVE text. Get the idea?	★ Decide what the *audience* is. This is the clue to what sort of language to include. E.g. *Write a letter to your best friend …* This tells you to use informal language because you know the audience well. *Write a report for the local museum on …* This tells you to use polite, formal language because you don't know exactly who will be reading it.
	ALWAYS READ THE QUESTION AT LEAST TWICE! Once you have decided on the purpose and audience, plan, write and check your writing.	

Recount

What kind of writing is it? Who is it for?
A recount gives information about something that has happened. You need to think about who the recount is for, because this will alter the tone you write in! A recount might be found in a newspaper. Biographies and autobiographies are also recounts.

Structure and language features
• *What structure should I use?*

Your plan might look like this:

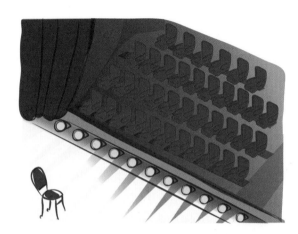

1 Start with an opening that sets the scene.

> *The other day, I went to the theatre.*
> (If it's a personal recount, you could start with a question to get your reader oriented.)
> *Did I ever tell you about the time I ...*

2 Paragraphs giving the events in the order they happened.

> *First we ...*

> *After that, we ...*

> *The last thing we did was ...*

3 Summary – try and round off your recount to help your reader understand what happened and why it was important.

> *I really enjoyed my day out, because ...*

• *What kind of vocabulary should I use?*
Use strong verbs and good descriptive language to bring your recount to life.
Use time connectives (see pages 38–39) to help your reader understand the order in which things happened.

To achieve Level 5 in a recount, you need to use:
• imaginative vocabulary
• a variety of sentences to get your meaning over clearly and interest your reader
• clearly organised paragraphs

A recount might look like this:

Our visit to the theatre

The other day, I went to the theatre with some friends. It was a big trip because the theatre was in Stratford-on-Avon, where William Shakespeare was born. It wasn't a play by Shakespeare we saw, though – it was a pantomime called *Beauty and the Beast*. It was wonderful!

- Who, what, when, where and why in first paragraph

- Personal opinion

We were staying in a hotel, so first we went there to check into our rooms and leave our bags. Then, full of excitement, we walked through the town to the theatre. There were lots of people around, all heading in the same direction. It seemed as if the whole world was going to see the play, which made us look forward to it even more.

- Use of time connective

- Phrase added for extra detail

- Time connective used again

Eventually, we got into the theatre through the crowds, and found our seats – very good ones, with a fantastic view of the stage. After a wait that seemed like ages, though it was really only a few minutes, the lights went down and the curtain went up.

- Complex sentence conveys lots of information quickly

Well, what can I say? The play was everything I'd hoped it would be. The girl playing Beauty was just right for a fairy tale heroine, and her wicked sisters were ugly and horrible, but very funny. There was a wonderful scene where the whole family had a mud fight, which all the children in the audience really loved (I did too!).

- You can use punctuation to add additional detail

But the best thing of all was the Beast. He was terrifying! He had huge claws and an enormous grizzled mane. His voice was echoing and his roar made everyone jump out of their skins. The most frightening thing of all was when he first came on, because he crawled headfirst down the wall of the stage! The little boy next to me hid his face in his dad's shoulder, and I didn't blame him.

- Last paragraph rounds off recount and refers back to subject

Of course, the Beast turned out to be the handsome prince, and he and Beauty got married and lived happily ever after. I was really sorry when it was all over – but I know I shall remember it happily ever after, too! It was the best theatre trip ever.

Practice questions

1 Think of a trip you've had, either with the school or with your family. Write a plan.

2 Now use your plan to write a recount of your trip.

Instructions and procedures

What kind of writing is this? Who is it for?
Instructions and procedures tell you how something is done, e.g. how to skateboard, how to make a cake.

Structure and language features
- *What structure should I use?*

Your plan might look like this:

1	What are these instructions for?	*How to make a model ship* *These instructions will show you how to ...*
2	A list of equipment and materials or ingredients. Try to put them in the order they're going to be needed.	*You will need:* *balsa wood* *glue*
3	A step-by-step account of what you need to do. You might use numbers or bullet points.	*1. Cut out the shape ...* *2. Place the ...* *3. Take the ...* *4. Finish off by ...*

Top tip
★ Sometimes, instructions or procedures are not written with numbers or bullet points. There is still the step-by-step approach but they are written as continuous prose. Quite a lot of recipes are written like this.

- *What tone should I use?*
  A formal tone is usually best. Use the *imperative voice* (see below).

- *What kind of vocabulary should I use?*
  Use time connectives, e.g. *first, then, next, finally.*
  Use technical vocabulary where appropriate – you might need to explain it.
  Give precise information about, for example, measurements, time, size and colour.

Grammar tip: The imperative voice
The imperative voice is what you use when you are giving instructions.
The verb comes at the beginning of the sentence, like this:
Put the mixture in the machine.
Take the cake out of the oven.
Make sure the wheels of your skateboard are running freely.

To achieve Level 5 in instructions and procedures, you need to:
- use words precisely
- convey meaning clearly

A set of instructions might look like this:

Chocolate sponge cake

Ingredients

For the cake

175 g margarine	1 tsp baking powder	
175 g caster sugar	5 tbsp cocoa powder	
150 g self-raising flour	3 eggs	
pinch of salt		

For the filling

jam or
chocolate spread

- Clear organisation with sub-headings
- Numbered points for clarity

Method

1. Preheat oven to 180 °C/350 °F/Gas 4.

2. Grease two 20 cm sandwich tins and line with greaseproof paper.

3. Cream margarine and sugar in large bowl.

4. Sift flour, salt, baking powder and cocoa into the bowl.

5. Add the eggs and mix carefully until the mixture is smooth.

6. Divide the mixture evenly between the tins.

7. Bake for 20–25 minutes until the cakes are springy to the touch and have left the edges of the tin.

8. Remove cakes from oven and allow to cool in tins for about 5 minutes. Turn out carefully onto cooling rack.

9. When cool, spread jam or chocolate spread on one cake and sandwich the other on top.

- Imperative (bossy) verb
- Action verb
- Adjective to assist reader
- Adverb to assist reader

Practice questions

1 Imagine you have an elderly aunt coming to stay. She is very independent and has insisted on finding her own way to your house. She says that all she needs is a clear set of instructions and perhaps a map to direct her to your home from the nearest station. Your writing task is to write her a letter that contains all the necessary information.

2 Look at the recipe example above. Can you change it from a set of instructions using steps into one that is a piece of continuous prose?

Check that your instructions are still clear when written like this – why not get someone to try out your recipe? See page 60 for answers.

Non-chronological report

What kind of writing is this? Who is it for?
A non-chronological report presents factual information in a clear and systematic way. The purpose of the report is to describe things *the way they are*. The people reading it (*the audience*) want to know the facts about your subject.

Structure and language features

● *What structure should I use?*

A new paragraph for each new idea. The paragraphs need to be in a logical order to make everything clear to your reader. Begin each paragraph with a sentence that will tell the reader what the paragraph is about. Start with the general, e.g. 'Volcanoes are … ' and move to the more specific, e.g. 'Mount Etna is … '.

Sum up your report in the last paragraph to round everything off.

Write your report in the present tense, unless it's about something that happened in the past.

> Your plan might look like this:

> *A volcano is a mountain or hill with a crater …*

1 Start with a paragraph defining what the report is about (introduction and general definition).

> **What happens when a volcano explodes (use technical vocabulary):**
> *Volcanoes explode when the magma …*

2 A new paragraph for each new idea. The paragraphs need to be in a logical order to make everything clear to your reader.
Start with the general and move to the more specific.

> **How volcanoes affect humans:**
> *Many volcanoes explode in remote areas, but some, like Mount Etna, …*

> *Volcanoes may seem frightening, but they have helped create the world we live in.*

3 Round off your report.

● *What tone should I use?*
Make it sound fairly formal – don't use slang or jokey language.
Don't use *I* or *we* or give opinions – try to stay neutral!
The *passive voice* is often useful (see next page).

● *What kind of vocabulary should I use?*
Use words that are factual and precise, descriptive but not imaginative.
Try to use:
● words that generalise, e.g. *mammals* rather than *some kinds of animals*, *public transport* rather than *buses and trains*
● some *appropriate* technical vocabulary

Grammar tip: The passive voice

Normally when we're writing, we say who does something in a sentence. *The dog ate the bone.*

In some kinds of writing, it's very useful not to do this. You would say instead: *The bone was eaten.*

This is a really good trick for making your writing sound more formal.

To achieve Level 5 in a non-chronological report, you need to be able to:

- convey meaning clearly
- use words precisely
- use a formal tone
- use complex sentences to explain ideas
- organise your work into paragraphs

A non-chronological report might look like this:

Sleep tight! A report on hibernation

When it gets cold in winter, human beings can turn the heating up, or wrap up warmly. Animals can't do this, so they have to find other ways of surviving. Some of them get through the winter by going into a deep sleep called 'hibernation'. The word hibernation actually comes from the Latin word for winter.

Animals hibernate for two main reasons. The first is that their bodies are not adapted to deal with deep cold. For example, reptiles, which are cold-blooded, need the warmth of the sun to give them energy to move and hunt their prey. Cold weather means that they cannot raise their body temperature high enough to move, so they hibernate until the warmth returns.

Animals also hibernate because their food supply runs out in the winter. Bats, for example, who feed on insects, would not survive in the cold weather when there are few insects to be found. Many other mammals hibernate for the same reason. These animals need to make sure they feed enough in the autumn to build up enough body fat to see them through without eating again till spring.

To hibernate means to go into a dormant or inactive state. When an animal hibernates, its heart rate and breathing go right down, so that it may almost seem to be dead. Its body temperature also goes right down. Because keeping warm takes a lot of energy, this is a very efficient way of conserving body fat.

When animals are hibernating, they are vulnerable to predators, so most hibernating animals find themselves a safe place to sleep away the winter. Hedgehogs roll up inside piles of dead leaves, bats hide away in attics or caves and dormice build nests at the base of trees. It's strange to think that if you walk through a wood in winter you may be very close to lots of hibernating animals, sleeping tight till spring comes!

- Title makes report sound interesting
- Introductory sentence
- Definition
- Additional comment to add interest
- New paragraph beginning to explain further
- Clear link to the first sentence
- Complex sentence giving lots of information
- Link to the last paragraph
- Word that generalises
- Technical vocabulary
- Specific examples
- Last sentence ties things up neatly by referring to the title

Practice questions

1 Use the four facts about Mount Etna below to write a paragraph in a report showing how volcanoes can be useful to us, even though they are dangerous. Try to use a variety of sentence types and link them with connectives like *however*.

Mount Etna is an active volcano on the coast of Sicily.
It is one of the most active volcanoes in the world.
Volcanic eruptions make the soil fertile.
There are many orchards and vineyards on the slopes of Mount Etna.
(See page 60 for an example.)

2 The table below gives facts about the speeds at which different animals can travel.

Write a report to tell your audience how humans compare with the speeds of other animals. Don't forget the following points.
- Have a plan and follow it.
- Put your paragraphs together logically, and link them where possible.
- Move from general points to specific examples.
- Use technical language where appropriate.

Animal	Typical speed	Special facts and features	What it eats
Cheetah	Over 100 kilometres an hour for short distances.	World's fastest runner. Built for speed with very long legs, special ridged foot pads that grip the ground, and a streamlined shape.	Grazing animals such as antelopes – needs to move fast to catch food.
Three-toed sloth	Can take a whole day to move 100 metres.	Slowest mammal in the world. Moving slowly may help it stay hidden from predators.	Leaves.
Human being	When walking, three to four kilometres an hour.	Fastest human runners can move at between 32 and 40 kilometres an hour. Like the cheetah, humans can only do this for short distances. Humans have invented lots of other ways of moving very fast.	Many different kinds of food. Humans used to hunt food, but nowadays are more likely to go shopping!
Swift	Measurement is difficult, but some experts believe they can fly at 160 kilometres an hour.	One of the world's fastest birds. Needs to fly fast to cover long distances as it migrates from Southern Africa to Europe and back again every year. Streamlined body and wings.	Fast-flying insects.

Explanation

Achieved?

What kind of writing is this? Who is it for?
An explanation tells the reader how something works or why things happen. It can be about natural things, e.g. *why volcanoes erupt*, or about mechanical things, e.g. *how a radio works.*

You would have to think about who your audience is to decide how complicated to make your explanation!

Structure and language features
• *What structure should I use?*

A plan for an explanation might look like this:

1 Tell the reader briefly what the explanation is about.

Why do birds migrate?

2 Paragraph describing parts and/or appearance of subject or process to be explained.

In the winter some birds fly south. Many make incredible journeys. Why do they do this?

3 Following paragraphs explain how the process works or what the object does in a logical sequence.

(You might use time connectives and/or connectives that explain why things happen (causal connectives) like because or so.)
Birds migrate in order to ...
Other reasons for migration are ...

4 Finish with a summing-up paragraph.

Migration is an amazing phenomenon ...

Use the present tense.

• *What tone should I use?*
An explanation should be written in a formal way.

• *What kind of vocabulary should I use?*
Use connectives that signal time.
Use technical vocabulary where appropriate.
Use connectives that show cause and effect, e.g. *because, as a result of this.*

To achieve Level 5 in an explanation, you need to be able to:
• convey meaning clearly
• organise paragraphs logically
• use a formal tone
• use words precisely

An explanation might look like this:

How do teeth work?

Most animals, including humans, grow two sets of teeth in a lifetime. The first set is called the milk teeth; the second is the permanent teeth. Teeth are used for cutting, tearing and grinding food. There are 20 milk teeth in a child's jaw and 32 in a full adult set. Each jaw has 4 biting teeth [incisors], 2 tearing and holding teeth [canines], 4 chewing and cutting teeth [bicuspids] and 6 grinding teeth [molars]. Teeth are made up of 3 parts: the crown [covered by hard enamel], the neck and the root [which holds the tooth in the jaw]. Underneath the hard enamel, the tooth is composed of dentine, which is a softer substance.

- Simple present tense
- Technical language
- Description of how teeth work

- Action verbs

When someone eats a piece of bread, their incisors bite into the bread and break off a small mouthful. Then their tongue moves the bread around the mouth so that the molars can grind the food into a pulp. This is helped by saliva that is produced in the mouth. This means that the bread becomes broken down into pieces that are small enough to swallow. Canines are used for tearing off tougher foods, like meat.

- Explanation of the process
- Connective
- Action verbs
- Cause and effect

- Summing-up paragraph

The different kinds of teeth work together to break down food so that it is easy to swallow.

Quick challenge

You have been asked to write an explanation. Make a list of five connective words or phrases you might find useful. See pages 38–39 for suggestions.

Write an explanation of 'How libraries work' using the following information to help you. Add more information if you can find it in a non-fiction book or encyclopedia but don't copy or include information you don't understand!

How do libraries work?

- Libraries hold stocks of books for the public to borrow or refer to.

- Non-fiction and fiction books are available.

- Most libraries have computerised systems, which are used for lending stock and locating particular books from other libraries in the area.

- To take out a book, a library card is needed. To get a library card you must take some proof that you live in the area.

- Every time you take out a book, the librarian will swipe the card and a bar code on the book on a machine. The machine records the title of the book, the date and your name.

- Plan your text using the steps on page 17.
- When you have completed your explanation, check it includes the language features – is it a Level 5 answer?

Discussion

What kind of writing is this? Who is it for?
A discussion text is sometimes called a balanced argument. It gives information about an issue from different points of view, and leaves you to make up your own mind.

Structure and language features
- *What structure should I use?*

A plan for a discussion might look like this:

1 State the issue and say what the main arguments are.

Should school lunches be made compulsory? There are arguments for and against. Some people say it would lead to children being healthier, while others are all for free choice.

You could do it like this. Group together all the arguments for the point of view and then group together all the arguments against it: Those who support the argument say ...

Or you could do it this way, presenting argument and counter-argument together: Those who support the argument say ... However, others point out that ...

2 Present arguments for and against the point of view. You can either put all the arguments for one viewpoint and then all the arguments for the other, or you can give argument followed by counter-argument, one point at a time.

They also point out that ... On the other hand, those against say ... Furthermore, they add ...

Another argument for this point of view is ... Again, others dispute this, saying ...

3 End with a conclusion, weighing up the evidence.

There are clearly sound points on either side. On balance, it seems ...

Use the present tense.

- *What tone should I use?*
Use an impersonal, formal tone, but you may choose to add personal comments in the conclusion.

- *What kind of vocabulary should I use?*
Use logical connectives such as *therefore, however*. Show how your discussion is unfolding by using connectives that order your ideas or add emphasis, like *in addition, furthermore*.
You can also use connectives which show that you are stating the opposite point of view, like *on the other hand*.
Move from the general to the specific, e.g. *Animals in zoos suffer ... Lions, in particular, ...*

To get Level 5 in a discussion, you need to show that you can:
- present ideas in depth and give several arguments for and against each viewpoint you are discussing
- use paragraphs logically
- use complex sentences to explain your ideas

A discussion might look like this:

Heelys – good news or bad?

One of the must-have toys of the last couple of years has been 'Heelys', the shoes with wheels in the heel that allow you to roll along smoothly by lifting your toes. Children love them, but an accident and emergency consultant has recently warned of the dangers of wearing them. So what are the facts?

Some shopping centres and stores in the UK have banned Heelys because they feel they are too dangerous. Representatives of some large supermarkets say that they do not allow Heelys either in their stores or in their carparks because of the dangers both to the wearers and to other shoppers. One spokesman said, 'It's all too easy for a child to lose control and collide with an elderly shopper, or get hit by a car. It's bad for the child and the rest of our customers, who have the right to shop in safety.'

Doctors also have safety concerns about the wheeled shoes. In just one month in one hospital, almost a dozen children have turned up with injuries after using Heelys. 'Some of the injuries are fractures which are really nasty,' said one doctor. 'These children are not wearing elbow pads or helmets, which would protect them at least slightly.' Indeed, one 12 year old was killed when he lost control of his Heelys and fell under a car.

The manufacturers advertise Heelys as a revolution in footwear, allowing the users to roll, walk or run. They say that many children can improve their balance and get enormous pleasure from wearing their Heelys, citing their enormous sales to prove this. They dispute the safety issue, saying that data proves that wearing Heelys is safer than taking part in nearly all other popular sports.

In contrast to the concern of doctors, the manufacturers point to the health benefits of using Heelys. Their chief executive said, 'In an age when childhood obesity is a worry, it's important for kids to be active and exercising, and our product encourages this.'

So there we have it – are Heelys a fun way of getting about and keeping healthy, or an accident-causing menace? What do you think?

- First paragraph introduces issue and gives preview of arguments for and against
- Introducing first argument against Heelys
- Quote gives additional weight to argument
- Introducing second argument against Heelys
- Evidence to back up viewpoint
- Further evidence – strongest argument last
- First paragraph supporting argument for Heelys
- Evidence to back up viewpoint
- Further evidence – using data to back up case
- Phrase linking with previous argument
- Second paragraph backing up arguments for viewpoint
- Summary of argument to round off discussion

Practice questions

1 The discussion about Heelys (opposite) is structured by stating all the arguments for one side first and then all the evidence for the other point of view. Can you rewrite just one paragraph so that it follows the structure of presenting one argument and its counter-argument together?

Use the blank spaces below to plan your answer.

Remember that you can use connecting words and phrases to introduce opposing ideas (e.g. *However, ...*; *On the other hand, ...*).

Planning notes

2 It has been suggested that your school should allow children to ride their scooters to school, and use them in the playground at breaktimes. Your school council has asked you to look into this and present the arguments for and against in the school newsletter so that parents and children can vote.

Don't forget, for Level 5 you need to have more than one argument for each viewpoint and back them up with evidence.

Planning notes

See pages 60 and 61 for answers.

Persuasion

What kind of writing is this? Who is it for?
A persuasive text is intended to convince the reader to do or think something. You need to think carefully about your audience in order to know how best to persuade them!

Structure and language features
* *What structure should I use?*

A plan for a persuasive text might look like this:

1 Opening statement (could be a question) presenting your argument.

Surely everybody knows that exercise is good for you?

2 Arguments to support your case, often an opening sentence backed up with more detail.

Exercise makes you feel good. This is because ...

Exercise also has undeniable health benefits. It has been proved that ...

3 Summary of key points and call to action.

In view of this overwhelming evidence ...
So what are you waiting for? Get exercising!

Top tip	★ Use the present tense, but you may need to use other tenses depending on the points you are making.

* *What tone should I use?*
  Use strong language to make your point – appeal to your readers' feelings. Consider your audience carefully and choose a formal or an informal style depending on the reader. A formal letter of complaint is going to be written very differently to a persuasive leaflet aimed at children.
  Rhetorical questions (that is, questions to which you don't really expect an answer) are very useful.
* *What kind of vocabulary should I use?*
  Use emotive words, that is, words to make your reader feel a particular way. E.g. *Smoking makes your breath smell revolting. It's a disgusting habit.*

To get **Level 5** in a persuasive text, you need to:
* use a variety of techniques to persuade, e.g. rhetorical questions, anticipating arguments against your point of view and countering them
* use complex sentences to explain your ideas

A persuasive text might look like this:

Give us a skateboard park!

Are you in favour of giving young people something to do, keeping them fit and keeping them off the streets? Surely the answer is yes. So why is our council blocking the building of a new skateboard park?

• **Rhetorical question to start**

For years, people in town have been disturbed by skateboarders using supermarket car parks and pedestrian precincts to practise their hobby. The skateboarders say that they have no wish to be anti-social in any way, but have no choice as they have nowhere else to go. Now they have been offered an ideal site on the outskirts of town, only to be thwarted by the council, who are refusing permission for the park to be built.

• **Stating the problem and the possible solution**

• **Emotive word**

Why? Skateboarding is healthy exercise, giving teenagers a chance to use up excess energy. Surely we'd prefer to see young people being active, not couch potatoes!

• **Presenting a positive argument**

Safety records are excellent and the organisers of the local skateboard club, who would run the site, say nobody will be allowed to skate without proper safety equipment. So the council cannot be refusing on safety grounds.

• **Anticipating and dealing with a possible counter-argument**

What's more, local skateboarders are planning to build the park themselves, with help from local businesses who are fully in favour of the project. This would mean that these young people would not only be helping themselves, but would also acquire useful skills for the future. The park would therefore not be a drain on council resources.

• **Anticipating and dealing with a possible counter-argument**

So are complaints from local residents at the root of the council's objection? On the contrary. Residents have in fact signed a petition supporting the park. 'We want to know our children have somewhere safe to go,' says a spokesperson. 'This park will be a valuable community asset.'

• **Use of connective phrase to signal counter-argument**

• **Anticipating and dealing with a possible counter-argument**

Safety measures, local agreement and business support are all in place – so what is the council's problem? Surely they cannot come up with any valid objection. Come on, give us our skatepark!

• **Summarising argument and finishing with call to action**

Practice questions

(1) Use the text above, and rewrite it to support the opposite point of view.

(2) Use the discussion text about Heelys on page 20 to write a persuasive text either for or against wearing them.

Writing fiction

Fiction texts can include stories, plays, poetry and other imaginative writing. The main purpose is to entertain your reader. Fiction can also inform, persuade or explain things.

In this section, we'll look at stories and plays. It's not very likely you'd be asked to write a poem in a test, though reading and writing them is good for your writing.

To achieve Level 5 in fiction writing, you need to be able to show that you can:
* choose and control the right structure
* use paragraphs to organise your writing
* make sensible links between and within paragraphs
* use a variety of sentence structures to add emphasis and convey meaning clearly
* use words precisely and imaginatively

Stories
There are several important types of story you might write. In your test, you might be asked to write either a story in the longer test, or a part of a story in the short test.

Quick challenge

See if you can match the sentences below to the right type of story:
Once upon a time, there lived a king and queen who longed for a child.
Herman was only small, but he was highly intelligent. He was also a hamster.
The robot moved silently towards the airlock.
Long, long ago, birds had no wings.
Now once there lived a little old woman in a little old house.
Her heart beating fast, Jo crept closer to the mysterious light in the woods.

**Myth   Fairy story   Humorous story   Science-fiction
Adventure story   Traditional tale**

It's important to start by working out what kind of story it is and who it's for – remember rule number 1:

What kind of writing is this? Who is it for?

When you know the answer to those questions, it will help you think about the particular kinds of characters, problems and language you would find in each of these kinds of stories.

Story structure

Stories have different features, but also lots of things in common. Here are some top tips for story writing.

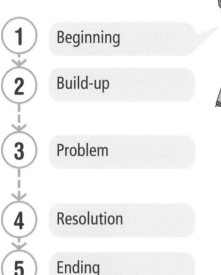

1 Beginning — **Introduce the setting and the main characters.**

2 Build-up — **The story gets going. The characters start to do something.**

3 Problem — **Something goes wrong!**
This is the most exciting part of the story.

4 Resolution — **The problem gets sorted out.**

5 Ending — **All the loose ends are tied up. The characters think or reflect on what has happened.**

This is a good starting point, but you don't have to stick to it like glue – for example, it's a good idea to start an adventure story in the middle of the action, and explain how your characters got there later.

Characters

Do not have too many characters in your story. Too many characters just get in the way – one, two or three main characters are enough, with one or two extras if you really need them.

It's much better to *show* what your characters are like than to spend ages describing them. A good way of doing this is through giving just a few details about their appearance.

In some kinds of story you don't even need to do this, because the characters are what's called *stereotypes*. For example, in fairy stories the witch is a baddie, the youngest son is the hero!

Quick challenge

Write three sentences describing the appearance of:
1. someone you want your reader to like and trust
2. someone you want your reader to be scared of
3. someone you want your reader to be not quite sure about

Dialogue

Dialogue means what people say to each other in stories or plays. It is another really important way of showing what your characters are like and a very good way of moving action on. The most important thing to remember about using dialogue, however, is DON'T USE TOO MUCH OF IT! It's all too easy to get stuck in a long conversation between two of your characters where the reader will get confused about who's saying what! Save dialogue for the times when it's really effective, like at the beginning of an adventure story.

Here's an example:
'This snow's brilliant!' yelled Rob, the minute he saw Jamie and Parminder in the distance.
'Fantastic,' grinned Jamie.
'And it means no school – so lots of time to work on our camp!' added Parminder.

These three lines of dialogue tell the reader who the main characters are, start to set the scene, and get the action going.

There are lots of strong verbs you can use for dialogue. Make sure you use them carefully so that they convey the meaning you want. Remember, to get Level 5, you need to use words precisely; scattering words like *muttered*, *yelled* and *exclaimed* around for no good reason is not a good idea. Use *said* if there's no cause to use anything different.

And don't forget – when you put in dialogue, you need to use speech marks and the punctuation that goes with them to make your meaning clear. Try using this checklist:
● *Have I started a new line for each new speaker?*
● *Have I put speech marks around what is actually said?*
● *Have I used the right punctuation with my speech marks?*

See pages 40–42 for more help with punctuation and dialogue.

Quick challenge

Write three lines of conversation between two friends at the beginning of a story agreeing to meet somewhere after school.

Setting

You don't need to give masses of detail to make settings real to your reader. A very good way is to describe a setting using the different senses: sight, sound, touch, smell, taste. Use two or three senses in one description of a setting.

Look at this description of a setting from a famous story:

Next moment she found that what was rubbing against her face and hands was no longer soft fur but something hard and rough and even prickly. 'Why, it is just like the branches of trees!' exclaimed Lucy. And then she saw that there was a light ahead of her; not a few inches away where the back of the wardrobe ought to have been, but a long way off. Something cold and soft was falling on her.

In this extract from *The Lion, the Witch and the Wardrobe*, CS Lewis uses the senses of touch and sight to describe Lucy's first discovery of the magical land of Narnia.

Quick challenge

Write a description of a scene in a classroom using three sentences and three senses! Make it sound dull and gloomy – a good start for an exciting adventure story!

Tips	★ A couple of final tips about settings: If you can, it's a good idea to write about a setting you know. Your back garden or street can be a great setting for an adventure story – you don't have to have your characters climbing Everest or diving down to the Titanic!
	★ If you are writing a short task that asks you to describe a setting, you can afford to put lots of details in. In a longer writing task, where the setting is just one of the story ingredients, you need to introduce the setting briefly. You can add more detail during the plot.

Planning

To achieve Level 5, planning your story quickly and efficiently is vital. Develop a way of planning that works for you and to stick to it. Here are the basic things you must think about:

- *Read the task carefully. What kind of writing is this? Who is it for?*
- What do you know about this kind of writing? What kind of setting, characters and plot belong in this kind of story?
- What shape will your story take? Use a five point plan (see page 25) to jot down the main points. Only write what you need in order to remember your ideas. Don't waste time writing whole sentences in your plan.
- Stick to your plan!

On the following pages are some examples of different kinds of story you may be asked to write, with their ingredients.

Adventure stories

Story structure

This could be quite simple, like this:

1	Beginning	Rob, Jamie, Parminder – day off school because of snow.
2	Build-up	Go to build camp in woods.
3	Problem	Get chased off by farmer. Hear cry for help – find farmer trapped by fallen tree.
4	Resolution	Rescue farmer who lets them play in woods whenever they like.
5	Ending	Tea and buns in farmhouse.

For Level 5, it could be better to use a rather more complicated structure, where you start in the middle of the action. A plan might look like this:

1	Problem	Sally and little brother Simon stuck on cliff with tide coming in.
2	Beginning	End of family holiday – last day.
3	Build-up	Sally and Simon wanting to go and have last look for dolphins off the beach.
4	Return to problem	Tide came in as they watched dolphins – trapped.
5	Resolution	Parents come round in boat and rescue them.
6	Ending	Dolphins lead parents to children.

This gives you a real chance to show how well you can handle the different parts of a story.

Characters and setting

It's best to keep the characters simple and like people you know. Remember, you don't usually need more than three people in this kind of story!

Keep the setting simple, too. You're most likely to be able to write well and quickly about the sort of places you know.

Other tips

★ To create an atmosphere of tension in your story, it's a good idea to use words and phrases that make your reader feel cold, e.g. *She froze in her tracks.*

★ It's also a good trick to use questions, e.g. *What was that? Why did it suddenly feel so cold?*

★ At Level 5, you must try to use different kinds of sentence in your writing. Short *simple* sentences add emphasis, while *complex* sentences give your reader lots of information quickly.

An adventure story might look like this:

Noises in the Night

Toby was petrified. He lay awake in the tent, listening to every rustle in the night. He knew he should never have agreed to this, but Josh had been so keen on the idea.

It had all started when Uncle Fred had been clearing out his garage and had found his and dad's old tents.

'Fancy camping again, Jim?' he'd joked with Toby and Josh's dad.

'Not on your life!' Dad said. 'I'm too old for that lark nowadays. We used to have fun though, didn't we, pretending to be explorers. Hey, boys – would you like to have the tents? You could camp in the garden tonight.'

'Cool!' yelled Josh, before Toby could say anything.

'OK,' he agreed, hoping he didn't look as unenthusiastic as he felt.

It was always the way. Josh was younger, but he always seemed to rush into things, and Dad teased Toby about his little brother being braver than him. So Toby often found himself saying yes to things he would prefer to have thought about first.

Now here he was, wrapped in a sleeping bag, lying wide awake in the middle of the night in the dark garden, and longing to be inside in his cosy bed. There was no light, not even the moon, and every little noise sounded frightening and unfriendly. He told himself that there couldn't possibly be anything worse than a hedgehog in the garden, and they weren't fierce, but – what was that? If that was a hedgehog, it was a giant one, and it was coming straight for Toby's tent! He screwed up his eyes and buried himself deep in his sleeping bag, barely daring to breathe as whatever it was came nearer and nearer.

'Toby,' said a little voice, 'can I come into your tent? I'm scared on my own!' Almost laughing with relief, Toby unzipped his tent to let in a very small and scared-looking Josh, wrapped in his sleeping bag.

'Come on, then,' he said. 'I'll look after you.' And they curled up and went to sleep. Before they knew it, it was morning, and Dad was bringing out bacon sandwiches. 'Well, Josh,' he said, 'were you scared?'

'Oh, no,' said Josh, 'I'm never scared when Toby's there. He's my big brother!' Toby took a huge mouthful of bacon sandwich. He felt great.

- Short sentence to start gives emphasis
- Setting established
- Starting with problem, getting right into the action
- Returning to beginning
- Dialogue used to move action on and establish character
- Build up – more about character of boys
- Return to problem
- Resolution
- Ending – Toby feels happy because Josh calls him brave

Challenge

Plan three adventure stories using these titles and ideas. Don't try and write the whole story at the moment, just get used to planning in under 10 minutes. Time yourself! Remember, keep it simple!

Around the corner You've just moved into a new house. As the previous owner drove away, he shouted something that sounded like, 'Don't go around the corner!' What happened?

Aunt Emma's visit Mum has had to go and look after gran and Aunt Emma is coming to look after Gina and her little sister Rosie. Gina wants everything to go really well so that her mum won't be worried. Rosie goes missing just as Aunt Emma is due.

Mum's new sari Dad has bought a beautiful new sari for mum as a birthday present. Devinder offers to pick it up on his way home from school, but then something happens ...

Now choose one of your plans and write the story – remember, stick to the plan and time yourself. You have 35 minutes.

Myths, legends and fables

Myths, legends and fables are not quite the same thing. You need to look closely at the task to decide if you're being asked to write one and if so, which one!

A **myth** is a story that's told to explain natural events like earthquakes or how things got to be the way they are.

A **legend** is a story told about people like Robin Hood or King Arthur. It may contain magical elements.

A **fable** is a story told to illustrate a moral, like *Cheats never prosper*. The characters are usually animals. One of the most famous fables is *The Hare and the Tortoise*.

How the rainbow got its colours

A plan for a myth might look like this:

1	Beginning. Set scene in an unspecified time and place, e.g. long ago, far away.	*In far-off times, the Sun God went out hunting.*
2	Problem	**Sun God puts down his bow and can't find it.**
3	Resolution	**Peacock promises to help him if he promises not to hunt birds. He paints bow so that it's easily found.**
4	Ending	*From that day to this, everyone can see the Sun God's bow whenever he leaves it in the sky.*

Characters and setting

The characters in a myth are often animals and/or gods. Natural forces such as fire, wind or volcanoes are represented as gods (remember, myths are stories told to help people explain things to themselves). Sometimes humans can be characters, but, if so, they are often referred to as just 'Man' or 'Woman', not by name as a specific person. Characters are good or bad!

The setting is usually not described in detail, just as an unspecified time and place, normally in the opening lines, which might look like these:
Long ago and far away …
In the distant days when no one can remember …
Back when the world was young …

Other tip	★ Try to use formal, story-telling language. These are the sort of stories made up to be told, not written down, so people use words and phrases that help them recall how the story goes. Repetition is often used to help with this.

A myth might look like this:

How the rainbow got its colours

Back when the world was young and all the colours were bright and new, the Sun God awoke one morning and stretched.

'I will go hunting,' said he. 'I will hunt out some tasty morsel and make a feast for my Lady Moon.' So he took his bow and his shining rain arrows and went out to hunt.

All day he hunted, but he had no luck. The birds and the animals heard him coming and hid themselves away, but they watched him through the leaves and from behind the trees. At last, as the dusk was falling, the Sun God threw down his bow in despair.

'I cannot catch anything,' he lamented. 'I will rest awhile and try again.' He sat down with his back against a tree.

In a little while he arose, feeling refreshed, and looked for his bow. But it was the same colour as the leaves on the ground, and look as he might, he could not find it.

'What shall I do?' he cried. 'If I cannot find my bow, I shall never be able to hunt again!'

At that very moment, there was a rustle from the bushes, and the most beautiful bird stepped out and stood before him. It was the wise old Peacock.

'I hear you, Sun God,' said Peacock, 'and I can help you, but I need your promise. If I help you, you must promise never to hunt another bird.'

The Sun God gave his promise, and Peacock spread his wonderful tail. Now a peacock's tail is covered in eyes, and in no time at all Peacock spied the Sun God's bow. The Sun God was delighted and he was even happier when Peacock took one of his own magnificent feathers and painted the bow with seven of his own beautiful colours.

'There,' said Peacock. 'Now you will never lose your bow again. But you must always keep your promise, because I shall be watching!'

And that is why, whenever the Sun God goes hunting with his shining rain arrows, you can see a rainbow in the sky. And that is why, to this day, peacocks have eyes on their tails – to make sure the Sun God doesn't forget his promise!

- Opening sets myth in some unspecified time
- Saying 'said he' rather than 'he said' makes it sound more formal
- Slightly old-fashioned language helps set the tone of the story
- Language of story-telling
- One animal standing for all

- Concluding paragraph explains natural phenomenon

Challenge

Using the story structure, and giving yourself time to plan, see if you can write a myth to explain one of the following:

How the Thunder got its Noise   *How the Tortoise got his Shell*
Why Birds have Wings

Playscripts

The key thing about playscripts is that **you have to tell the story and show character mostly through dialogue**. The structure of the story you tell, however, will usually be the same as the story plans we've already looked at!

Playscripts can be a bit tricky, because there are two audiences you need to keep in mind. You need to think about your actors – the people who might be acting your play – and how to make it clear to them what they should be doing and saying. You also need to think about the people who will be watching your play, and telling the story so that they really enjoy it.

Special kinds of playscript

Sometimes you might be asked to write a playscript for a particular purpose, e.g. for a television advert. Remember rule number 1: *What kind of writing is this? Who is it for?* That will help you think about other things you need to include.

How to set out a playscript

* You may need to start with a list of the characters in your play, and a very short description of them. (This depends on what task you've been set, so read the instructions carefully!)
  Characters:
  Mum, who has broken her leg
  Dad
  Joe, aged 11
  Chelsea, his little sister, aged 5

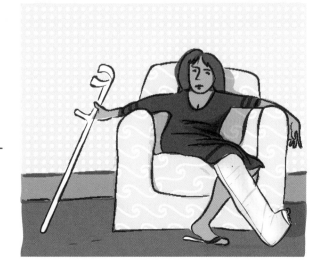

* You can include a short description of the setting. This can be written in note form – you don't need to write in complete sentences.
  The scene is the living room in Joe's house. Mum is sitting on a chair with her leg in plaster.

* Put the name of the character speaking on the left, and separate it from what is actually said with a space. You can write the characters' names in capital letters if you like, or put a colon (like this :) after the characters' names. It doesn't matter, so long as you're consistent! The point is to make sure that the actors who might use your playscript don't get confused between their names and what they're supposed to say!
  Mum: *Joe!*
  Joe: *Yes, Mum?*

- Stage directions (what you need to tell your actors to do) should be put in brackets if you are writing your play by hand. If you are using a word processor, you can put them in italics. Again, the point is to make it clear to your actors what they're meant to do, and to stop them getting it mixed up with what they're supposed to say. Either way, keep stage directions short!

Chelsea: *(Sobbing)   I can't reach!*

Characters and settings

Playscripts will be based on a particular type of story (e.g. an adventure story), so characters and settings in playscripts will be the same as they would be if you were writing that kind of story!

Dialogue

Of course, dialogue is the key part of a playscript, and you have to make it not only tell the story but also show what your characters are like. Think about the sorts of ways particular people might speak, and try to use dialogue to show this to your audience.

Witch: *Hee, hee, I have you now, my precious!*
Small child: *Want bunny now!*
Teacher: *Michael, I really don't think rocking on your chair is a good idea, do you?*

Quick challenge

Write a line of dialogue showing how the following people might speak.
A policeman   A sinister man   A grandmother

Challenge

Your school has been chosen for a healthy eating project by a celebrity chef. Your class has worked with him to invent a new menu for school meals, and now you are trying to persuade other children to have school dinners instead of packed lunches. Write a script for an 'advert' to be performed to the school in assembly. Remember: *What kind of writing is this?*

Grammar

Polishing up your grammar could make the final difference to your writing.

Being clever with sentences

To achieve Level 5, you need to use different types of sentence and punctuate them correctly. Always remember rule number 1: *What kind of writing is this? Who is it for?* This will help you decide what kind of sentence is best at any point in your writing.

Top tips	★ *Think it, say it, write it, read it!*
	★ Get into the habit of continually rereading what you've written. This will help you avoid silly mistakes and make sure you've said exactly what you meant.

Sentences start with a capital letter and end with a full stop (.), question mark (?) or exclamation mark (!).

Quick challenge

Read through a piece of writing you've done recently. Have you got all the capital letters, full stops, question marks and exclamation marks in place?

Three types of sentence

There are three main types of sentence: *simple*, *compound* and *complex*. You can use them to have different effects on your reader. See below for help!

Simple sentences

Don't be fooled by the name – *simple* sentences aren't necessarily easy!

A simple sentence has one verb, which means there is one *clause*. A main clause makes sense on its own.

The following are both simple sentences:

It was raining.
He's really looking forward to his birthday tomorrow!

Short simple sentences are especially good to use
- in stories, echoing the action: *She stopped.   He ran.*
- in non-fiction, to introduce paragraphs or new ideas:
  The swift is one of the world's fastest birds.

However, using lots of simple sentences can be very boring for a reader, especially if you don't vary the length.

I went out. It was raining hard. I put up my brolly. I saw my friend Daisy. I called loudly to her. She came over.

Quick challenge

Turn these six simple sentences into two compound sentences using any combination of *and*, *but*, *or*, *so*.

I went out. It was raining hard.
I put up my brolly. I saw my friend Daisy. I called loudly to her. She came over.

Compound sentences

Compound sentences are made up of one or more simple sentences joined by one of these four *connectives*:   and   but   so   or

It was raining hard <u>so</u> I put up my brolly.
We can go out <u>or</u> we can stay in.
Heelys are dangerous <u>and</u> they cause accidents.
Heelys are dangerous <u>but</u> children love them.

Compound sentences can be especially useful when you want to give your reader additional information while still sounding neutral.

Complex sentences

A *complex sentence* is one where there is one main clause and one or more *subordinate clauses*. Remember, a main clause makes sense on its own. A subordinate clause does not make sense on its own.

   I put up my brolly because it was raining.
   (Main clause)   (Subordinate clause)

Complex sentences are often made by using a *connective* word or phrase (see page 38 for more help with connectives), like those below:

   after   although   as   because   before   if   in case
   once   since   though   unless   until   when   while

These connectives often help you show the order in which things happened or cause and effect, so this kind of complex sentence is particularly useful in non-fiction writing.

Another way of constructing a complex sentence is by dropping a subordinate clause into a main clause, like this:

   Jenny, *who was trembling,* opened the door.

This kind of complex sentence is particularly good for conveying a lot of information in a small space, so it is especially useful in fiction writing. JK Rowling is very good at this!

It is possible for different kinds of sentence to be combined, like this:

   He ran down the road and flung himself on the bus, while the sinister man stood watching at the corner.

To be sure of getting Level 5, you have to be able to:
* choose the right kind of sentence for what you want to say
* use a good variety of sentences
* link them sensibly so your reader can follow your train of thought easily

Ways of varying sentences

Mixing types of sentences

Challenge

Read the following paragraph from a non-fiction text. Use three different colours to highlight the different kinds of sentence.

Many birds migrate. Some fly only a short way each year, but others travel enormous distances. They do this because they need to feed and raise their young. Many birds eat insects, which vanish in cold weather. As their food sources disappear, birds need to find new ones.

Now write a non-fiction paragraph about a different animal using the same pattern of sentences.

Different sentence starts

You can start your sentences in different ways. Starting with a connective phrase or a subordinate clause is a good trick to vary your writing.

Turning nervously, he saw the teacher.
On the other hand, you could look at it like this.
Although Heelys are fun, they are incredibly dangerous.

Using questions

In stories, you can have your character asking questions when they are speaking but try asking questions in other parts of the story, too.

Hanif could just see something through the mist, but what was it?
Why was the table shaking?
How would Jake get out of this fix?

Asking questions means that the reader also asks them and becomes more interested in the story.

You can use questions in non-fiction, too. They are especially useful in persuasive writing and discussion.

Using exclamation marks

One exclamation mark at a time is enough! Using two or three just looks silly and isn't Level 5.

Top tip	★ Look at books in your classroom and find examples of how authors use different sentence types in their writing. Try using some of their sentences as models for your own writing.

Organisation

Remember you need to organise your writing into paragraphs.

Paragraphs help writers put their ideas in order and help readers to follow the storyline, argument or dialogue.

Level 5 writers are able to use paragraphs to present their work logically and fluently.

For the writing tasks you will have a planning sheet which you can use to help structure your work. It usually prompts ideas for paragraphing.

Whilst writing, it is really important to put your pen down and reread what you have written. By doing this you can check if:

★ you need to start a new paragraph

★ your ideas are connected

★ your writing makes sense.

If you find there are gaps, or a paragraph is too long, insert a note NP (new paragraph) so that the marker knows this is a new paragraph.

In **non-fiction**, starting a new paragraph shows the reader that *PERSON*, *PLACE*, *TIME* or *TOPIC* has changed.

This means that:
• when a new subject (*PERSON*, *PLACE* or *TOPIC*) is introduced, you begin a new paragraph
• when *TIME* moves backwards or forwards, you begin a new paragraph

In **fiction** you also start a new paragraph when *PERSON*, *PLACE*, *TIME* or *TOPIC* has changed.

This means that:
• when you change the setting (*PLACE*), you begin a new paragraph
• when a new character (*PERSON*) is introduced, you begin a new paragraph
• when there is a change of speaker (*PERSON*), you begin a new paragraph
• when *TIME* moves backwards or forwards, you begin a new paragraph
• when a new event (*TOPIC*) happens, you begin a new paragraph

Top tip	★ Think PPTT (PERSON, PLACE, TIME, TOPIC) for starting a new paragraph.

Quick challenge

Read two pages of a non-fiction book. At the end of each paragraph, make a note of the main focus. How is the writer moving the writing on? Do the same with a fiction book.

Types of connectives

To be a Level 5 writer, one of the most important things you need to do is make sensible links between your sentences and your paragraphs, so your work flows logically and smoothly.

Sometimes you need to help your reader see the connections between your sentences and paragraphs, and you do this by using *connectives*. Connectives are words or phrases that link clauses and sentences or introduce new paragraphs.

Level 5 writers use a range of connectives accurately and fluently. Look carefully at the range of connectives available for you to select from and use.

Adding connectives – to add extra information	Sequencing connectives – to show time passing, instructions
• and • also • as well as • moreover • too	• next • then • first, second, third… • finally • meanwhile • eventually • after • before
Emphasising connectives – stress emphasis, arguments, persuasion	**Comparing connectives – to compare ideas, arguments, discussion**
• above all • in particular • especially • significantly • indeed • notably	• equally • in the same way • similarly • likewise • as with • like

There are different connectives for different purposes.

Cause and effect connectives – explanations, arguments, reports	Qualifying connectives – to show a conditional clause
• because • so • therefore • thus • consequently	• however • although • unless • except • if • as long as
Illustrating connectives – arguments, persuasion	Contrasting connectives – to compare, discussion, arguments
• for example • such as • for instance • as revealed by • in the case of	• whereas • instead of • alternatively • otherwise • unlike • on the other hand

Top tip

★ If you do not fully understand how to use a connective, use another one with which you are confident. In this example, the connectives used do not make sense:

Keith had great fun at the zoo, *on the other hand* he had ice-cream whereas he watched the monkeys eating *as revealed by* a great day out.

Quick challenge

Choose the most appropriate connectives from the list below to link the following pairs of sentences. Remember, you use some connectives to make two sentences into one, and others to make links between sentences.

Some people say Heelys should be banned. Other people do not agree.
Heelys should be banned. They are dangerous.
The day began well. It got worse and worse.
Exercise is good for you. Everyone should do more.
Sarah was scared. She opened the door.

but   because   however   although   therefore

Higher-level punctuation

Level 5 writers use a range of punctuation accurately and purposefully. This means using a wide range of higher-level punctuation, without forgetting to use more common features such as full stops, commas and capital letters.

When writing, it is tempting to try and impress by using brackets, dashes, colons and all sorts of other Level 5 features. However, if you do not use them correctly, this may happen:

Claire really enjoyed swimming with (her best friends) at the local sports centre. They usually went; every Saturday morning – it cost £2 each although – during the school holidays they could use their, discount cards.

Quick challenge

Rewrite the above paragraph using brackets, dashes and a semi-colon accurately. You will need to add some extra information for it to make sense.

To add extra information	brackets, dashes or commas	Safa's teacher (Miss Richens) always dressed in style.
		Safa's teacher – Miss Richens – always dressed in style.
		Safa's teacher, Miss Richens, always dressed in style.
To introduce a list	colon	The school tuck shop will now sell: carrot sticks, toast, yoghurts and a variety of fresh fruit.
To separate single items in a list	commas	They helped themselves to tea, coffee, cream cakes and chocolates.
To separate clauses	commas	Even though it was pouring down, we went to the park.
To separate phrases or clauses	semi-colon	It is important to eat a balanced diet: carbohydrates which give you energy; proteins to help growth; fibre to aid digestion and some fats to act as an energy store.

Speech punctuation

There are two ways of telling a reader what a character says:

- Indirect speech
  This is also known as 'reported' speech, when you don't use the speakers' exact words but report what they said.
  > *The teacher threatened to give extra homework if their work did not improve.*
  > *The doctor told me how he had saved her life.*

- Direct speech
  You can use the speaker's actual words inside speech marks (' ') but there is a bit more punctuation needed!

The most common punctuation is a comma. Here the comma is used at the end of the spoken words INSIDE the speech marks.
> *'We are going to have a wonderful time,' he announced.*

If the speaker continues talking, you need another comma before the next spoken words.
> *'We are going to have a wonderful time,' he announced, 'and everyone will take part!'*

If you start the sentence with the speaker and speech verb, the comma comes before the speech mark and the speech begins with a capital letter.
> *Flora said, 'You don't have to go.'*

Full stops, exclamation marks and question marks must be placed inside the speech marks.
> *'I'm not going!' she yelled.*

And finally: new speaker = new line.
> *'I'm not going!' she yelled.*
> *'Why not?' asked Mr Parker.*

Quick challenge

Punctuate the following dialogue:

Hey said Fred what about giving me a hand with this piano. I can't replied Bob. Why not Fred demanded. Because I'm underneath it said Bob.

Top tips	★ Notice that when the speech verb comes in the middle of one continuous sentence, the second group of words inside speech marks do <u>not</u> need a capital letter to begin them.
	★ The speech verb or pronoun after the spoken word always begins with a lower case letter, while a PROPER NOUN begins with a capital letter: *'Rubbish!' she said.* *'Rubbish!' answered Mary.* *'Rubbish!' Mary cried.*

Apostrophes

Take special care with apostrophes! They can change the meaning of a sentence when used badly.

There are only two reasons why you need an apostrophe:
* to show that a letter or letters have been missed out (omission)
* to show that something belongs to somebody (possession)

> You never need an apostrophe for anything else!

Omission

Sometimes a letter (or part of a word) is missed out to make a shortened form. You put an apostrophe in where the letters are missed out. This often occurs in direct speech so that it sounds natural.
E.g. *Could not* becomes *Couldn't*   *Was not* becomes *Wasn't*

Possession

You use an apostrophe to show possession, that is, that something belongs to someone.
* *The boy's homework* (showing that the homework belongs to the boy)

Be careful with plural nouns (more than one):
* *The boy's boots* (the boots belonging to one boy)
* *The boys' boots* (the boots belonging to two or more boys)

Don't be fooled by words ending in *s*, like *princess*:
* *The princess's crown* (the crown belonging to the princess)
* *The princesses' crowns* (the crowns belonging to the princesses)

Top tips	★ *It* – this is the really tricky one. Learn the rule and you won't make mistakes!
	★ The apostrophe is ONLY EVER used with it when a letter is missed out (the shortened form).
	★ *It is a great adventure* becomes *It's a great adventure.*
	★ The apostrophe is NEVER EVER used to show possession with *it.*
	★ NEVER EVER use an apostrophe with plural nouns UNLESS it shows possession.

Other Level 5 punctuation

To achieve Level 5, you must show the use of other punctuation that **adds voice** to your writing. Try using the following:

* Colon (:) Two dots, one above the other. Used to introduce a list.
  The following are all mammals: cow, dog, human.

* Ellipsis (…) Three dots. Used to show there is a long pause or something is missed out.
  'It's gone …' her voice trailed off, as she realised the implications of the loss.

* Dash (–) Shown as a line. Used to add an afterthought.
  My great aunt was evil and – there's really no polite way to put this – smelly.

Choosing words for effect

When choosing vocabulary, remember, every word counts!

- Vocabulary choices need to be precise, accurate and imaginative.

- Choosing words is like telling jokes: even the best shouldn't be used too often or they will lose their impact.

Adjectives

Definition

Adjectives come before or after a noun; they describe somebody or something. They can create powerful descriptions but you must take care not to overuse them and to use them accurately.

The verb *fought* creates a powerful picture, gripping the reader's attention.

The cliffs *fought* with the waves from the **rippling sea**, roaring to be successful.

Rippling is not a good adjective!
More accurate alternatives might be:
- **rough**
- **choppy**
- **storm-tossed**

- You should never use two adjectives with the same meaning in one phrase, e.g. *The rough, bumpy path*

- Two adjectives may be used if they both add useful detail to the story, e.g. *The steep, rough path* OR *The lonely, rough path* (Two very different paths!)

★ Danger! Never use common adjectives, e.g. *okay, great, really, boring*, from speech in your writing unless they are quotes or in dialogue.

Dolphins are really interesting is not a good sentence.
Dolphins are fascinating is a Level 5 description!

- An accurate noun is often better than a string of adjectives or an adjectival phrase. *The doctor, who was going to perform the operation, strode into the room.* would be better as … *The surgeon strode into the room.*

- Adjectives work well when they alliterate (start with the same sound), e.g. *The dark, dense, dank branches brushed brutally against his face.*

Practice question

1 Turn these into appropriate written sentences by changing the underlined adjective.

a) The news was <u>pretty boring</u>.

b) I watched a <u>great</u> movie last night.

c) The uniform was <u>okay</u> but the hat didn't fit.

d) The shop was full of <u>really great</u> clothes.

Adverbs

Definition

Adverbs can be used to tell how something was done.

The old man climbed <u>slowly</u> and <u>painfully</u> up the winding stairs.

Practice questions

Improve these sentences with adverbs.

a) Anna poured the hot tea [ ].

b) The car was reversed [ ] into the drive.

c) The ducks swam [ ] on the polluted pond.

d) On the count of four she leaped [ ] onto the box.

Verbs

- Clear and interesting writing is often achieved through the use of powerful verbs.

    Jack jumped up and rapidly pulled tins and packets out of the cupboard.
  OR
    Jack jumped up and rummaged through the cupboards.

  The second sentence would be the choice of a Level 5 writer!

- Don't tell the reader what to feel; make them feel it themselves through the description. Look how many verbs David Almond used to create this powerful description in his book *Skellig*:

The door creaked and cracked a moment before it was still. Dust poured through the torch beam. Something scratched and scuttled in the corner. I tiptoed further in and felt spider webs breaking on my brow.

Tip	★ It's not necessary to use phrases like *It was scary* if your descriptions are powerful enough. Your description makes suggestions for the reader's mind to work on.

Figurative language

Here are some more useful vocabulary choices.

Repetition

This is a useful tool for building atmosphere or suspense. Repetition often works well in short phrases.

> *Fog everywhere. Fog up the river, fog down the river. Fog on the Essex marshes, fog on the Kentish heights. Fog in the eyes and throats of the Greenwich pensioners wheezing by the firesides.*
>
> From *Bleak House* by Charles Dickens

Simile

This creates an image in the reader's mind by comparing a subject to something else. The comparison is often made by using the words AS or LIKE and frequently exaggerates.

> *It was as if the fires of the sun burned in his face.*
>
> *Her eyes sparkled like sunlight on water.*

Metaphor

This describes a subject by writing as if it really is something else. A metaphor can sound stronger than a simile.

> *The twins were a hurricane leaving a trail of destruction behind them.*
>
> *A river of tears streamed down the old woman's face.*

Draw up a table like this and keep a record of any interesting vocabulary you could use in your writing. Learn the definitions of the words and how to spell them.

Verbs	Adverbs	Nouns	Adjectives

Spelling

The spelling test lasts 15 minutes. You will be asked to spell 20 words in sentences that your teacher reads to you.

The test will cover:
* basic spelling rules
* more difficult or unusual words that might not fit basic spelling rules

Spelling rules

The spelling rules that follow will help you. Read through and make sure you understand them. Then remember to use them when you write.

Plurals

* Most words just add *s*.
    road – roads; cup – cups; book – books; cat – cats

* Some words need *es* to be added. Say them aloud and listen to how they sound. Words that end in a hissing or buzzing sound follow this rule. Words that end in *x, z, ch, sh* and *s* also follow this pattern.
    Box – boxes; bus – buses; watch – watches

* Words that end in *f* have a different pattern. You usually need to drop the *f* and add *ves*. *Hoof – hooves; wolf – wolves*
    But beware! There are exceptions. Try to learn these words.
    Gulf – gulfs; roof – roofs; dwarf – dwarfs/dwarves

* Words that end in *y* have a simple rule: If the letter before *y* is a vowel (*a e i o u*), just add *s*.
    Way – ways; toy – toys; monkey – monkeys
    If any other letter (a consonant) comes before the *y*, drop the *y* and add *ies*.
    Lady – ladies; spy – spies; story – stories

* Learn the irregular words.
    Mouse – mice; man – men; child – children
    When you are reading, make a note of any irregular plurals you find and learn them.

Challenge

Look through books or dictionaries and find words ending in *y, x, z* and *s*. Change them into plurals.

Practice question

Change these words into plurals:

fox, road, bunch, wish, sound, life, tax, tree, drink, pirate, house, donkey, fly, bus

Adding suffixes -er, -ed or -ing

There is a simple way to understand how to spell words that end in a consonant when you add -er, -ed or -ing. Listen to the sound the vowel makes.

Vowels can make short sounds or long sounds.
Stop has a short 'o' sound.   *Boat* has a long 'o' sound.

The rule is: double the consonant when the vowel is short.
Stop – stopping   *Boat – boating*

Quick challenge 1

1. Divide these words into two lists. Put all the words with short vowel sounds in one list, and all the words with long vowel sounds in the other list.
    bin, line, paper, chat, choose, flutter, reign, wet, meet, light, float, dot

2. Look through some books and add four new words to each list.

3. Add an -er, -ed or -ing ending to the words to make a different word.

4. Check the vowel sound to see which words need to have a double consonant.

5. Check your spelling in a dictionary.

Tricky words

'i before e except after c when the word rhymes with bee'

- When words have a long 'ee' sound and are spelled with *i* and *e*, the *i* comes before the *e*: *achieve, believe, thief*. But there are exceptions to this rule.

- If the long 'ee' sound (*i* and *e*) comes after the letter *c*, then the reverse happens – the *e* comes before the *i*: *receipt, deceive, perceive*

- There are other words that do not follow the rule and you should learn them: *weird, weir, seize*

- Whenever you find an example while you are reading, write it down and learn it.

Quick challenge 2

Tenses: Put these verbs into the past, present and future tenses. It is a good way to practise many of the spelling rules. If you find spelling some of them hard, look back at the spelling rules and learn them. If you still have trouble getting them right, read as much as you can and practise all you can. Check your answers on page 63.

- To fit
- To keep
- To produce
- To move
- To swim
- To try
- To clap
- To fly
- To pursue

Reviewing your work

Rereading or reviewing your work is an important part of being a writer. No writer thinks their work is finished without rereading it and checking it makes sense. Don't worry if you find things that need changing – there are always changes to be made. It is a good opportunity to look at ways in which your writing could be improved.

Here are some ideas to keep in mind when you are reviewing your work.

- **Make sure your reader will understand your main message**. For example, if you are writing a mystery story, will your reader want to find out what happens? Ask yourself if you have given too many clues to the ending. Is there a feeling of suspense and excitement? If you are writing an explanation, have you used connectives to help your reader follow the process that you are explaining? Would you be able to understand the explanation easily? If you are not sure, have another look at the guidelines for writing explanations.
- **Make sure you have followed the guidelines for the text type you are writing**. If you are not sure, go back and check. Keep the style constant and try not to slip from one type of writing to another. If you have started in the first person voice, have you kept to it all the way through your writing? Have you kept to the same verb tense? Don't get worried if you find mistakes – just correct them and try to remember for the future. No one gets it right all the time, but reviewing your work helps you to spot the errors that could lose you marks.
- **Check your spelling and grammar**. Look carefully as you read and, if a word doesn't look right, try it out a few times on a piece of paper. If you can, look it up in a dictionary and try to learn the correct spelling for the future. Read your sentences aloud. This will help you to hear when something doesn't sound right. When you think your grammar is not quite right, try saying the sentence in different ways and rewrite it a few times. Pick the one that you think sounds best and don't be afraid to make changes. Go back and check for any simple mistakes. Have you added all your capital letters and full stops?

Checklist
1. Is your main message clear?
2. Have you followed the guidelines for the text type you are writing?
3. Is your style consistent?
4. Have you used the same verb tense?
5. Have you checked your spelling and grammar?

Writing and reading skills

Did you know that teachers are helping you develop your **writing** in at least eight ways? These are called 'assessment focuses' (AFs) and they are described here.

AF	Teacher language	This means...
1	Write imaginative, interesting and thoughtful texts	My writing is imaginative, interesting and thoughtful
2	Produce texts which are appropriate to the task, reader and purpose	I am able to write for different purposes and audiences according to the task set
3	Organise and present whole texts effectively, sequencing and structuring information, ideas and events	I can plan my writing and produce texts that sequence ideas, information and events within an appropriate structure
4	Construct paragraphs and use cohesion within and between paragraphs	I can use topic sentences and linking sentences to guide my reader through the text
5	Vary sentences for clarity, purpose and effect	I can use different types of sentences – simple, compound and complex – according to purpose and to create specific effects
6	Write with technical accuracy of syntax and punctuation in phrases, clauses and sentences	I am able to use different types of punctuation to make the meaning clear to my reader
7	Select appropriate and effective vocabulary	I can select and use a range of vocabulary, making choices according to purpose and audience
8	Use correct spelling	I can spell accurately

Reading is not just about being able to say and understand the words you see. Reading skills include the different ways you are expected to respond to a text. The seven assessment focuses for reading are:

AF	Teacher language	This means...
1	Use a range of strategies, including accurate decoding of text, to read for meaning	I can read for meaning
2	Understand, describe, select or retrieve information, events or ideas from texts and use quotations and references from texts	I can understand and pick out the appropriate quote, event or idea from a text and use PEE (Point, Evidence, Explain) to demonstrate my understanding
3	Deduce, infer or interpret information, events or ideas from texts	I can read and understand meaning that is only hinted at
4	Identify and comment on the structure and organisation of texts, including grammatical and presentational features at text level	I can identify the text type according to its presentational features and conventions. I can also comment on the writer's choice of text type to suit purpose
5	Explain and comment on the writer's use of language, including grammatical and literary features at word and sentence level	I can explain why the writer has made certain language choices (imperative verbs, emotive language, figurative language, formal/informal etc.)
6	Identify and comment on writers' purposes and viewpoints and the overall effect of a text on the reader	I can identify the writer's purpose and viewpoint and comment on how this affects the reader
7	Relate texts to their social, cultural and historical contexts and literary traditions	I can see how texts fit into their cultural and historical traditions

Reading comprehension

Achieved?

The Reading Test comes in the form of two booklets – one containing the texts you will read and another with the questions and space for your answers.

You have 60 minutes to read the booklets and answer all the questions.

Reading the texts

Read the text in the booklet. DON'T RUSH. Make sure you read the contents page. It has key information which prepares you for the types of texts you will be reading, e.g.:

If there are words you don't understand, read on and perhaps the paragraph will make sense anyway.

> DON'T RUSH!

> A country of colour – a brief summary of how South Africa has changed in recent years.

The questions

Always read the question carefully before you write. Look at the top of the page; it will tell you which section of the reading booklet you need to look at. There are different types of questions which you will begin to recognise. Some questions:

★ require a short answer, for example *who, what, when* style questions

★ require a longer answer, for example *why, how, do you think* questions

★ involve no writing at all, but instead you will need to circle the right answer, tick some boxes or match up ideas

★ might ask you about how a text is organised – pictures, subheadings, text in boxes, bold print, etc.

★ ask for your opinions and views – remember to link these to the text.

The reading test consists of different types of questions. Some of them are easy to answer (the information is right there) and some require you to apply some higher-level thinking skills. These are the Level 5 questions.

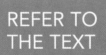

> REFER TO THE TEXT

This table will help you to recognise the question types and identify how to answer them.

Type of question	How to recognise them	Skills needed
Literal	Who, what, when?	Answer is usually right there in text
Inference	Why, how?	'Read between the lines', what is hinted at
Deduction	Do you think?	Find evidence, clues to support you
Evaluation	Explain why…	Explain what makes something effective, successful, etc…
Authorial intent	The author uses… What is the effect of this?	Explain why the writer made these choices

Answering the questions

After you have read the question, look across in the margin and you will see how many marks the question is worth (these usually range from 1 to 3 marks). This should help you to structure your answer. You must REFER TO THE TEXT in your answers. You can read the reading booklet as many times as you want! Although some of the questions require deep thinking, the answers will always relate to the reading booklet.

Reading between the lines

Authors do not tell the reader everything. Through action, description and dialogue they show many aspects of the story. When reading a passage, you have to work out what it is saying. You have to read between the lines.

Here are three examples to help you:

1 She stared wistfully into the shop window.

There is something she would like to buy or own but probably cannot BECAUSE that's what wistfully staring into a shop window usually implies.

2 Pulling on his hat, scarf and woollen gloves, he strode off into the night.

It's cold outside BECAUSE people wear hats, gloves and scarves in the cold.

3 Mina knelt down to welcome Fido, who came bounding up the path and covered her face with warm, loving licks.

Mina already knows this dog and knows it's friendly BECAUSE people do not usually allow unfamiliar dogs to come close to their face or indeed cover them with licks.

Read between the lines and try to work out what is really being said.

Text 1 (Fiction)

Bootleg
This extract has been taken from a novel called *Bootleg* by Alex Shearer.

It is set in the future when 'The Good For You' political party is running the country and forcing everyone to lead healthier lives. Chocolate addicts Smudger and Huntly watch in horror as their favourite food is swept from the shops and so-called Chocolate Troopers arrest anyone caught with sweets. The boys discover the recipe for chocolate and begin to fight back with their secret operation.

As the boys suspected, having the sugar thermometer made the crucial difference. Finally they could get the mixture to the absolutely precise temperature and keep it there for the given time. They could see as they poured the warm mixture out into the cooling tray that it was starting to congeal immediately. It didn't even have to go into the fridge. The boys just sat and watched, fanning the chocolate gently with empty sugar bags.

'I reckon we've done it,' Huntly said quietly. 'I'm not one to leap before he looks or who counts his horses before they've hatched, but look at that.'

The mixture went on changing, becoming hard and smooth.

'You make a note of the proportions?' Smudger asked.

Huntly pushed a piece of paper across the table.

'There. They were right all along. It was all in the temperature, like we thought.'

'You make a note of the cooking time too?'

'Yeah,' Huntly said. 'All the facts.'

'Good,' Smudger said. 'Then we're in business.'

His eyes lit up with sudden inspiration. He went into the stockroom and returned with a packet of raisins and a box of hazelnuts.

'What's that for?' Huntly asked.

'For the next batch,' Smudger said. 'What do you reckon? How about some fruit and nut!'

Huntly's face lit up with a smile.

'You're on, Smudge. Let's get to it.'

By the time Mrs Bubby woke from her nap, there were three trays of chocolate in the kitchen – plain, fruit and nut, and plain again – and they had cooled sufficiently to be cut into squares and wrapped.

After first expressing her admiration (and accepting a little taste of each) she fetched a sharp knife, a roll of cooking foil and her kitchen scales.

'Ok. I'll cut, you two weigh and wrap,' she said. 'We'll try to get as near as we can to 125 gram bars, as that's what people are used to. We'll wrap the plain chocolate in cooking foil with the shiny side out. And we'll wrap the fruit and nut with the shiny side in. That way we can tell at a glance which is which.'

The chocolate was soon cut and wrapped and stacked neatly into small cardboard boxes – of which Mrs Bubby had plenty.

'One hundred and twenty bars, Mrs Bubby,' Smudger said. 'A nice even number. Eighty plain, forty fruit and nut. Oh and ...' he looked down at the table where three (shiny side out) chocolate bars lay '... three left over.'

'Well, now that is untidy,' Mrs Bubby said.' And I do so hate an odd number. What could we do with them?'

'Give them to charity?' Huntly suggested.

'Not a bad idea,' Mrs Bubby agreed. 'But maybe a bit too risky these days. You know what? I think we should have one each.'

And they did.

Practice questions

If you need more space for your answers use extra paper.

1 What did the boys fan the chocolate with?

_____

_____

AF2 [ ] 1

1 mark

2 Find and copy **two** quotations which show that this wasn't the first time the boys had tried to make the chocolate.

_____

_____

AF3 [ ] 2

2 marks

3 'Huntly's face lit up with a smile'. Why was he so happy?

_____

_____

AF3 [ ] 3

2 marks

4 Using the text to support your answer, why do you think it was important for the boys to weigh the chocolate before they wrapped it?

_____

_____

_____

AF3 [ ] 4

2 marks

5 What is the purpose of the use of the ellipsis … in the paragraph beginning One hundred and twenty bars, Mrs Bubby?

_____

_____

AF4 [ ] 5

2 marks

6 In this extract Smudger acts like the leader. Find **three** pieces of evidence from the text to support this.

_____

_____

_____

AF3 [ ] 6

3 marks

Total marks [ ]

53

Text 2 (Playscript)

'Round the Cauldron' from *Macbeth*
William Shakespeare
In this scene, three witches are making a magic potion in their cauldron (a large metal pot for cooking). Some words are defined in the glossary under the text. The column on the right of the text tells you which sound effects goes with which line.
Sound effect 1: Wind sounds
Sound effect 2: Owls hooting
Sound effect 3: Dogs howling

First witch:	Thrice the brinded cat hath mewed.	1
Second witch:	Thrice, and once the hedge-pig whined.	1
Third witch:	Harpier cries "'Tis time, 'tis time!"	1
First witch:	Round about the cauldron go;	2
	In the poisoned entrails throw.	2
Second witch:	Toad, that under cold stone	2
	Days and nights has thirty-one	3
Third witch:	Sweltered venom sleeping got	3
	Boil thou first i' th' charmèd pot.	3
All:	Double, double toil and trouble;	1 & 3
	Fire burn, and cauldron bubble.	1 & 3
First witch:	Fillet of a fenny snake	2
	In the cauldron boil and bake.	2
Second witch:	Eye of newt and toe of frog,	2
	Wool of bat and tongue of dog,	1
Third witch:	Adder's fork and blindworm's sting,	1
	Lizard's leg and howlet's wing,	1
First witch:	For a charm of powerful trouble,	2
	Like a hell-broth boil and bubble.	1
All:	Double, double toil and trouble;	2 & 3
	Fire burn, and cauldron bubble.	2 & 3
Second witch:	Scale of dragon, tooth of wolf,	3
Third witch:	Witch's mummy, maw and gulf	3
First witch:	Of the ravined salt-sea shark,	1
Second witch:	Root of hemlock, digged i' th' dark	1
Third witch:	Add thereto a tiger's chaudron	2
	For th' ingredience of our cauldron.	2
All:	Double, double toil and trouble;	1-2-3
	Fire burn, and cauldron bubble.	1-2-3

Glossary

brinded – with the streaked fur
harpier – the god harpier
fillet of a fenny – fillet of a snake that lived in a bog
howlet – a young owl
maw and gulf – a gulf like stomach
ravined – of the rough sea salt glistened

hemlock – poisonous plant
tiger's chaudron – tiger's guts

Practice questions

If you need more space for your answers use extra paper.

1 In the extract different parts of animals are used. Match the animal name and the relevant parts.

Animal name	Part of animal
dog	eye
newt	tooth
wolf	tongue

AF2

1

2 marks

2 The three witches recite 'Double, double toil and trouble; Fire burn, and cauldron bubble,' three times in this short act. What do you think is the effect of this?

_____

_____

_____

AF4

2

2 marks

3 Explain what you think is the purpose of including sound effects.

_____

_____

_____

AF5

3

2 marks

4 List **two** ways that show how the layout of this text helps readers to understand when to read their part.

_____

_____

AF4

4

2 marks

5 Find and copy **three** pairs of rhyming words from the text.

_____

_____

_____

AF5

5

3 marks

Total marks

Text 3 (Poetry)

The Send-off

This poem is set in World War 1 and describes men leaving their homes to fight as soldiers.

Down the close, darkening lanes they sang their way
To the siding-shed,
And lined the train with faces grimly gay.

Their breasts were stuck all white with wreath and spray
As men's are, dead.

Dull porters watched them, and a casual tramp
Stood staring hard,
Sorry to miss them from the upland camp.
Then, unmoved, signals nodded, and a lamp
Winked to the guard.

So secretly, like wrongs hushed-up, they went.
They were not ours:
We never heard to which front these were sent.

Nor there if they yet mock what women meant
Who gave them flowers.

Shall they return to beatings of great bells
In wild trainloads?
A few, a few, too few for drums and yells,
May creep back, silent, to still village wells
Up half-known roads.

Wilfred Owen

Glossary

siding-shed – a railway shed at the end of a track where goods are usually loaded
   from, not men
gay – cheerful
spray – women gave men flowers as they left for war
porters – people who work at the station, carrying luggage
front – frontline in a battle
great bells – church bells rang when soldiers returned

Practice questions

If you need more space for your answers use extra paper.

1 Owen writes 'signals nodded' as if the train signals are people telling the train driver to leave. Find and write down **one** other phrase where it seems that objects are secretly helping to send the soldiers off to war.

_____

AF3

1

1 mark

2 From the first few lines explain how you think the men might have been feeling as they (a) marched to the station and (b) when they were on board the train.

(a) _____

(b) _____

AF3

2

2 marks

3 Owen describes the number of returning soldiers as 'a few, a few, too few for drums and yells'. What is the effect of this line?

_____

_____

AF5

3

2 marks

4 Owen suggests the men 'may creep back, silent'. What does this suggest about their state of mind?

_____

_____

AF3

4

2 marks

5 Using this poem, explain what you think is Owen's opinion of war.

_____

_____

_____

_____

AF6

5

3 marks

Total marks

Handwriting

Handwriting is teacher assessed as part of wider writing assessment. Do your best to always keep your handwriting neat and easy to read!

The golden rules

- Space out words and sentences evenly.
- Write on the lines if you are using lined paper.
- Use a pen or pencil you feel comfortable with and always use an eraser to rub out mistakes.
- Keep the letters the same size.
- Write so everyone can read your writing!

Example: 1

If your handwriting looks like this, you need to work on:

- joining up letters so they flow together neatly
- keeping the letters the same size
- spacing out the letters evenly. Some of these words are quite squashed!

Once upon a time, long ago there was a princess. She was the most beutiful princess in the world. Her dress sparkled as much as her charming atitude. She was the happiest prettiest person in the world.

Example: 2

If your handwriting looks like this, you need to work on:

- making sure all, not just some, of the letters are joined together
- getting the ascenders (the upward parts of letters like d and b) to face the same direction.

Once upon a time, long ago there was a princess. She was the most beautiful princess in all the land. Her dress sparkled as much as her charming attitude. She was the happiest, prettiest person in the world.

Overall, the shape and size of the letters are even and the writing is easy to read.

Example: 3

The letters are all correctly formed and are evenly sized and spaced. The other good thing about this handwriting is that it has its own style, so try to develop a style of your own.

Once upon a time, long ago there was a princess. She was the most beautiful princess in all the land. Her dress sparkled as much as her charming attitude. She was the happiest, prettiest person in the world.

Hints and tips	★ Compare a sample of your handwriting with the ones on this page. Which one is it most like? What are you doing well? What do you need to work on to make it better?
	★ Go over what needs improving with a highlighter pen, then rewrite the same sample, making as many improvements as you can.
	★ Practise a few sentences at a time, rewriting them and making improvements.
	★ Try especially hard to join the letters – it really speeds up writing!

Glossary

Adjectives words that add information or description to nouns

Adverbs words that add information or description to verbs

Cause what makes something happen

Character someone in a story; what someone is like, personality

Comprehension understanding

Conclusion the end of something; the resulting idea or thought about something

Connectives words that are used to link sentences and paragraphs

Deduction the use of evidence in the text to work out what the author is telling you, to read *between* the lines

Dialogue the words spoken by characters in a story

Effect the result of something happening

Emotive appealing to the emotions

Evidence something that proves what you think or believe

Fiction stories that are imagined, not real

Imperative verbs that give a command, e.g. *Go* or *Put*

Inference the use of your own knowledge *and* the evidence in the text to come to a conclusion about what the author means, to read *beyond* the lines

Issue a matter or subject for discussion

Logical resulting naturally

Non-fiction texts that give you information

Omission missing out

Paragraphs a number of sentences grouped together, usually linked by idea, topic, time, place or theme

Passive voice a verb form where the action is done by someone else, e.g. *it was thrown*. The 'opposite' of this is the **active voice**, where the subject of the sentence does the action, e.g. *he threw it*

Possession owning

Problem something that goes wrong

Proper noun a noun that names a person, place or organisation

Recommendation what you think should be done

Resolution how a problem is sorted out

Review look back at critically or carefully

Setting where a story takes place

Stereotype a character, usually in a fairy story or traditional tale, who has no real distinguishing characteristics, e.g. *a bad witch, a handsome prince*

Summary a short piece of writing that sums up the main points

Theme an idea that a story or poem is about

Answers

Page 11 – Recount: Practice questions 2

Did you remember:

• an opening paragraph that sets the scene and tells you when, why, where, who?

• paragraphs telling events in the order they happened?

• some detail to make it interesting for the reader?

• a closing paragraph to round it all off?

How long did it take you? Did you have time to check it over and make sure you hadn't made any daft mistakes?

Page 13 – Instructions and procedures: Practice questions 2

Here's an example of what your recipe might look like as a piece of continuous prose.

> ### Chocolate sponge cake
>
> To make this delicious cake, you will need the following:
>
> 175 g margarine
> 175 g caster sugar
> 150 g self-raising flour
> 1 tbsp cocoa powder
> 3 eggs
>
> pinch of salt
> 1 tsp baking powder
>
> For the filling, you'll need jam or chocolate spread.
>
> First, put the oven on at 180 °C/350 °F/Gas 4. While it is heating up, grease two 20 cm sandwich tins and line them with greaseproof paper.
>
> To make the cake, cream the margarine and sugar together in a large bowl, and then add the flour, salt, baking powder and cocoa, sifting them. Add the eggs and mix them in carefully. You should end up with a smooth mixture. Divide this equally between the tins. Bake the cakes for about 20–25 minutes until they feel springy to the touch and have left the edges of the tin. Allow them to cool for about five minutes and then turn them out carefully onto a cooling rack. When they are cool, spread one of them with jam or chocolate spread and sandwich them together.

Your instructions don't have to look exactly like this, so long as it's clear to the reader what to do!

Page 16 – Non-chronological report: Practice questions 1

Your paragraph might look something like this:

Even though they can be very dangerous, volcanoes are often useful to humans. Mount Etna is an active volcano on the coast of Sicily and it is one of the most active volcanoes in the world. In spite of this, however, there are many orchards and vineyards on its slopes, because the frequent eruptions make the soil fertile.

- Starting your sentence with a subordinate clause is a good way to vary your writing
- Two key pieces of information in a compound sentence
- Connectives linking this sentence with the previous one and making the connection clear

Page 18 – Explanation: Quick challenge

You might use any of these connective words or phrases:

This is because	In order that	So that	As a result of this
Because	This causes	So	Then
Next	Finally	Consequently	

There are others – how many could you think of?

Page 21 – Discussion: Practice questions 1

Here's one way you could do this:

Doctors also have safety concerns about the wheeled shoes. In just one month in one hospital, almost a dozen children have turned up with injuries after using Heelys. 'Some of the injuries are fractures which are really nasty,' said one doctor. 'These children are not wearing elbow pads or helmets, which would protect them at least slightly.' In contrast to the concern of doctors, the manufacturers point to the health benefits of using Heelys. Their chief executive said, 'In an age when childhood obesity is a worry, it's important for kids to be active and exercising, and our product encourages this.'

Page 24 – Writing fiction: Quick challenge
Match the sentences to the story type:
Once upon a time, there lived a king and queen who longed for a child.   Fairy story
Herman was only small, but he was highly intelligent. He was also a hamster.
   Humorous story
The robot moved silently towards the airlock.   Science-fiction
Long, long ago, birds had no wings.   Myth
Now once there lived a little old woman in a little old house.   Traditional tale
Her heart beating fast, Jo crept closer to the mysterious light in the woods.
   Adventure story

Page 35 – Sentences: Quick challenge
You might do it like this:
I went out, but it was raining hard, so I put up my brolly. I saw my friend Daisy and called loudly to her, so she came over.

Page 36 – Sentences: Challenge
Many birds migrate. Some fly only a short way each year, but others travel enormous distances. They do this because they need to feed and raise their young. Many birds eat insects, which vanish in cold weather. As their food sources disappear, birds need to find new ones.

Yellow = simple   Red = compound   Blue = complex

Page 39 – Connectives: Quick challenge
This is the best way of using these connectives:
Some people say Heelys should be banned but other people do not agree.
Heelys should be banned because they are dangerous.
The day began well. However, it got worse and worse.
Exercise is good for you. Therefore everyone should do more.
Although Sarah was scared, she opened the door.

Page 40 – Higher-level punctuation: Quick challenge
Claire really enjoyed swimming – with her friends – at the local sports centre. They usually went every Saturday morning; it cost £2 each. During the school holidays, however, they could use their discount cards (which meant it cost £1.50 each instead).

Page 41 – Speech punctuation: Quick challenge
'Hey,' said Fred, 'what about giving me a hand with this piano?'
'I can't,' replied Bob.
'Why not?' Fred demanded.
'Because I'm underneath it!' said Bob.

Page 46 – Spelling: Challenge
foxes, roads, bunches, wishes, sounds, lives, taxes, trees, drinks, pirates, houses, donkeys, flies, buses

Page 47 – Spelling: Quick challenge 2

Verb	Past tense	Present tense	Future tense
To fit	I fitted I have fitted I was fitting	I fit I am fitting	I will fit
To move	I moved I have moved I was moving	I move I am moving	I will move
To clap	I clapped I have clapped I was clapping	I clap I am clapping	I will clap
To keep	I kept I have kept I was keeping	I keep I am keeping	I will keep
To swim	I swam I have swum I was swimming	I swim I am swimming	I will swim
To fly	I flew I have flown I was flying	I fly I am flying	I will fly
To produce	I produced I have produced I was producing	I produce I am producing	I will produce
To try	I tried I have tried I was trying	I try I am trying	I will try
To pursue	I pursued I have pursued I was pursuing	I pursue I am pursuing	I will pursue

Pages 52–53 Text 1 (Fiction): *Bootleg*

1. Empty sugar bags.

2. Any **two** of the following: *'having the sugar thermometer made the crucial difference'*, *'Finally they could get the mixture'* and *'It was all in the temperature, like we thought.'*

3. Because Huntly had found raisins and hazelnuts to make 'fruit and nut' chocolate *(1 mark)* and this really excited him *(1 mark)*.

4. Either:
   To make sure that each piece was 125 g *(1 mark)*; so that they were all fair. *(1 mark)*
   This was the normal size for chocolate bars *(1 mark)* and people were used to this. *(1 mark)*

5. The ellipsis shows a passing of time. *(1 mark)* An additional mark awarded for an explanation: when Smudger looks down at the chocolate, which he wants to eat, before he looks back up at Mrs Bubby to hear her answer.

6. Smudger decides to make fruit and nut *(1 mark)*; he checks with Huntly if he has made a note of the proportions and cooking times *(1 mark)*; he takes responsibility for counting the chocolate. *(1 mark)*

Pages 54–55 – Text 2 (Playscript): 'Round the Cauldron', from *Macbeth*

1. Eye of a newt, tongue of a dog and tooth of a wolf.

2. Any two of the following *(1 mark each)*: The witches are working as a trio as they throw their ingredients in separately; they chant in unison; they dance around the cauldron; it shows that they are in this together.

3. Any two of the following *(1 mark each)*: This is to help children to enhance the performance of this scene; children may not have musical instruments or computer sounds so they can make these sound effects to enhance their performance; to entertain the audience; to build up atmosphere.

4. Any two of the following *(1 mark each)*: When a new character speak their lines are on a new line; set out clearly with the character's name and a colon; names are bold and in capitals to stand out.

5. Any three of these pairs:
   Sweltered venom sleeping got/Boil thou first i' th' charmèd pot;
   Double, double toil and trouble/Fire burn, and cauldron bubble;
   Fillet of a fenny snake/ In the cauldron boil and bake;
   Eye of newt and toe of frog/ Wool of bat and tongue of dog;
   Adder's fork and blindworm's sting/ Lizard's leg and howlet's wing;
   Scale of dragon, tooth of wolf/ Witch's mummy, maw and gulf;
   Of the ravined salt-sea shark/Root of hemlock, digged i' th' dark;
   Add thereto a tiger's chaudron/ For th' ingredience of our cauldron.

Pages 56–57 Text 3 (Poetry): *The Send-off*

1. 'A lamp winked to the guard.'

2. (a) Happy/carefree: singing as they left; (b) worried, try to look OK on the outside, on the inside frightened.

3. *1 mark awarded for each reason:* To emphasise that not many soldiers will return, many of the soldiers who are sent will die; There will be no celebration for the few who do return 'no drums and yells'.

4. One mark awarded for each of the following: They may be unsure whether their families will be there; Worried if their families will be proud of them; They may be injured and unable to walk.

5. *1 mark for each of the following:* Owen thinks war is pointless, a send-off should be a happy time but this is like sending men off to be slaughtered and killed. War generates paranoia – the soldiers think that even the streetlights are in conspiracy against them. Many men won't come back – too few – and will they be welcomed and helped to settle back in to society?